# The Blizzard Voices
# by Ted Kooser

WITH A NEW INTRODUCTION BY THE AUTHOR

ILLUSTRATIONS BY TOM POHRT

University of Nebraska Press
Lincoln and London

First Nebraska paperback printing: 2006

The Bison Books edition of *The Blizzard Voices* is
reproduced from proofs of the letterpress printed
limited edition published by The Bieler Press in 1986.

Library of Congress Cataloging-in-Publication Data
Kooser, Ted.
The blizzard voices / Ted Kooser, with a new introduction
by the author; illustrations by Tom Pohrt.
p. cm.
ISBN-13: 978-0-8032-5963-8 (pbk.: alk. paper)
ISBN-10: 0-8032-5963-8 (pbk.: alk. paper)
1. Blizzards—Nebraska—Poetry. 2. Nebraska—History—
19th century—Poetry. I. Title.
PS3561.O6B58   2006
811'.54—dc22    2006009134

# Introduction

The poems that follow are isolated voices heard in that blinding snowstorm we know as the passage of time. When the Alberta Clipper, roaring out of the north, rips apart a straw stack, only the frozen center remains, and each of these memories is like that center, stripped of digression, picked clean of equivocation. What is left are the core narratives, spare and cold. Each clings to a concrete and specific detail, for memory works like that. Recall gets snagged on some sharp thing, like a cornshuck on a barbed wire fence. Someone remembers the pets spinning around and around as the barometer dropped. Another remembers the row of sunflower stalks that she and her schoolmates followed to safety.

I snagged these poems from actual reminiscences, recorded in old age, of people who survived the most talked about storm in American history, the Blizzard of 1888, also known as the Schoolchildren's Blizzard because of the many children and their teachers who were trapped in rural schools on the bitterly cold days of January 12 and 13 of that year. In the Nebraska State Capitol, near the ceiling of the Great Hall, is an abstract mosaic, mostly blue and white like a snowstorm, dedicated to one of those teachers, Minnie Mae Freeman, who led her students to safety, trailing hand in hand through the blinding snow. Minnie's voice as I imagined it appears in this book.

My sources are many. When I was a boy there were people in my family, then in their seventies and eighties and nineties, who remembered the Great Blizzard and would from time to time talk about their experiences. I was bound by their spell as only a child can be. All my life I have been talking with people about their experiences of the great storm. Preparing to write these poems, I read town and county histories that mention the blizzard. W. H. O'Gara's book *In All its Fury*, published in 1947 by

Union College Press, is a superb collection of memories of the storm, and I used it extensively as a resource, as have other writers. But these poems are wholly mine, trimmed and shaped and imagined by me. I took the straws snagged on the fence and froze my own stories around them.

This book was performed as a play by the Lincoln, Nebraska, Community Playhouse in the late 1980s, and what struck me most was not the pleasure of seeing my work come to life but what occurred in the theater lobby afterward. Somehow my poems and a handful of talented actors had set memory free, and as I walked through the crowd with my cup of punch I overheard things like, "Well, my grandmother told me . . ." and "Great Uncle Harry once said that . . ." It was one of the most marvelous evenings of my life, for what I'd written was being put to service, and a community was awakening to a history they'd misplaced until those costumed figures in lantern light showed how to find it again. Out came the memories, all whispers and awe, and those recollections blew around in a swirl in that lobby until they once again caught up on the barbs of time. Once again our ancestors groped through the darkness for that row of sunflower stalks that might lead them into the next day and the next. And there we followed. I have rarely been more deeply honored.

*To the memory of my uncle, Alva Bert Moser*

## A Woman's Voice:

Eighteen eighty-eight, a Thursday,
the twelfth of January:
It had been warm all morning,
with a soft, southerly breeze
melting the snowdrifts back
from the roads. There were bobwhite
and prairie chickens out
pecking for grit in the wheel-ruts.
On lines near shacks and soddies,
women were airing their bedding—
bright quilts that flapped and billowed,
ticks sodden as thunderheads.
In the muddy schoolyards, children
were rolling the wet gray snow
into men, into fortresses,
laughing and splashing about
in their shirtsleeves. Their teachers
stood in the doorways and watched.

Odd weather for January;
a low line of clouds in the north;
too warm, too easy. And the air

filled with electricity;
an iron poker held up
close to a stovepipe would spark,
and a comb drawn through the hair
would crackle. One woman said
she'd had to use a stick of wood
to open her oven door.

## A Man's Voice:

Father and I had pulled the pump up
out of the well to put
new leathers in the cylinders.
I looked toward the house and saw
that our cats were spinning around
and around on the steps
as if they were drunk. Then the air
was suddenly full of snow,
weeds, dust and fodder, blowing
out of the northwest. We ran in
and pulled the door shut, snapping
the bottom hinge in the wind.
A wall of snow hit the house
and shook it hard, and it grew dark
as night. We had plenty of coal
to burn, for Father had bought a load
the week before. Through the night,
the house rocked like a cradle,
cracking much of the plaster loose.
In the morning we found

the wind had packed the snow so hard
our horses could walk on it
without breaking the crust.
The drifts were there till June.

## A Man's Voice:

One man who was lost that day
had been shelling corn, and had gone
to a neighbor's to borrow
a grain scoop. Halfway home,
he was caught by the storm,
and he left the scoop in the snow
near the road. He wandered
ahead of the wind and was found
that spring when it thawed, twelve miles
southeast of his home.

## A Woman's Voice:

My Henry was cutting ice
on the Platte with a good-sized
crew of men from Cozad. Mules
pulled the marker and plows,
and the men did the sawing.
Others floated the blocks
to the bank and loaded them
onto the wagons. The banks
were so high the crew didn't see
the blizzard coming until
it was right on top of them.
They could hardly force the mules,
four span of them, to face
into the storm. The wind
was so bad the men took turns
at the driving while others
laid in the wagon boxes.
None of them died, but some lost
fingers and toes that day.

## A Woman's Voice:

My maiden name was Hanna,
and I was twelve at the time.
We had been playing Fox-and-Geese
in the schoolyard, during
the afternoon recess,
when the blizzard bore down
out of the northwest, roaring
and whistling, loud as a train.
There was lightning in front,
and it looked like bales of cotton
twenty-five feet high, tied up
with flashing silver wire.
I shall never forget that night,
as we stood close by the stove
in that creaking, drafty schoolhouse,
doing our best to comfort
the little ones, who were cold
and afraid of the darkness.
We sang all the songs we knew,
including "Blow winter winds,
as hard as you will; we shall
be gay and happy still."

## A Man's Voice:

I had been to the schoolhouse
to see if the children were safe.
We decided they should stay
where they were, for they had coal
enough for the night, and food—
biscuits a neighbor had baked
and spread with molasses,
and a pail of hot coffee.
I started out riding for home,
but finally had to lead
the horse, who was blinded.
Once he opened his mouth
and the wind choked him
so that he fell. I got him

over against a strawstack
and left him there for the night,
and made it to home on foot
by following a fence-line.

## A Woman's Voice:

I didn't like our teacher,
and often got in trouble
for little or nothing.
She'd have me standing for hours.
On the day of the blizzard,
I was just standing there
when the first blast shook the school
and blew the stoveout. Without
dropping one stitch of that lesson,
she turned to me and said,
"Nettie, you may sit down."

# A Man's Voice:

Depending where on the plains
you were that day, there was between
eight inches and a foot of snow
fresh on the ground. From all accounts,
the blizzard picked it up
and ground it fine to a powder,
then added another foot
of new snow to it. The drifts
on the morning after the storm
were twenty and thirty feet deep.
In one low draw, a windmill
thirty-five feet high was covered
clear up to the topmost blades.
Houses and barns were buried,
and one man found his soddy
by falling in through the roof.
The temperature dropped
from just above freezing, at three,
to fifty below the next morning.

## A Woman's Voice:

I was an Ohio girl
who taught in a country school.
How I remember that day!
When the blizzard hit, it blew
some of the shutters closed
with a bang, breaking some panes,
and the snow came pouring in.
Toward evening, our fuel was gone,
so we set out walking,
holding each other's hands.
It was impossible to see,
but we followed a row
of dead sunflower stalks

all the way to a nearby farm.
I never see a sunflower now
that I don't count my lucky stars.

## A Man's Voice:

Father had plowed a fire-guard
alongside the house and barn
the previous fall. When the fence
played out, we followed the guard
by crawling along and feeling
the clods with our hands. I lost
some fingers, but was lucky;
they found my Uncle Silas
frozen standing upright
between two of his horses.

## A Man's Voice:

Corn was at twelve cents a bushel,
a good deal cheaper than coal,
so we fed our stoves with corn
and, sometimes, with twists of hay
or cowchips. Some folks had
the new Hay-Burner stoves
that would burn all night on one twist,
but not us. On the night
that the big storm struck, we burned
the floorboards from the side-porch
and some of the furniture
because we couldn't reach the barn
for fuel. My sister was born
about two in the morning
with my grandmother tending
my mother. We pinned up quilts
and sheets along the walls
and over the bed to keep the snow
off Mother and the baby.

## A Woman's Voice:

That morning, the sun had been out
and bright, and the new snow
sparkled like diamonds. At noon,
I noticed a cast of thin clouds
to the west, and a rainbow
completely around the sun.
We had a span of streetcar mules
which we'd bought in Omaha
to break the sod with. My Lewis
had taken them to get a load
of buckwheat flour at the mill
and bring it back to the store
that we kept in those days.
When the storm hit, I knew he'd
never get back that night,
so I tied a clothesline
out to the cobhouse and back
and brought in cobs to burn.

All night the wind moaned and cried,
but we were safe by the stove,
my Otto, who was seven;
my Laurie, who was five;
and my little Susan, just three.

## A Man's Voice:

We older students went home
at noon to help cut cornstalks,
for the weather was fine.
The storm caught us out in the field,
but we made it back to the house.
My father was ill, and sent me
out to feed our horses. That wind
was so strong it took the straw
out of my hands as fast as I
could pull it out of the sack.

## A Woman's Voice:

According to weather reports
at the time, the storm front moved
southeasterly, sweeping
the blizzard before it.
The mercury plummeted—
sixty degrees at some stations.
Railroad travel was blocked,
and telegraph clerks
sitting in boxcars rocked by wind
on the sidetracks tapped out
the news. The tight wires whined
along the tracks past schoolyards
where children played, black clouds
piling up over their shoulders.

## A Man's Voice:

One of the Holverson boys
thought he could make it over
to a neighboring house
to bring back food and blankets.
He put on two of our coats
and a scarf around his face.
We had some rags that we used
to wipe the blackboards off
which we tied around his wrists
and ankles. Out he went,
vanishing into the storm
a few feet from the building.
All of us children took turns
standing out in the entry,
beating on pails and pans
to guide him over and back.
He brought back all the blankets

those people could spare, and a tin
of beef. He was so tired,
when he stumbled back to us,
that he couldn't speak for an hour.

## A Woman's Voice:

How the good Lord, in his
infinite mercy, let those
poor little children die,
I'll never understand.
Not only were there freezings,
but fires. One house in town
burned right to the ground
when the wind sucked the flames
up into the chimney,
and one of the boys died
when the roof fell in on him.

## A Woman's Voice:

In all my years I never saw
another thing like that storm.
When it came it felt as if
an enormous fist had struck
the house. Snow fine as flour
sifted in under the eaves
and piled along the walls.
Our youngest, Jim, was at school
on a place two miles above,
and we were worried sick
for fear he'd try to get home
and be lost. You couldn't see
your hand at the end of your arm
out in it. My husband led
one of the horses up the lane
but had to turn back. The snow
had frozen the horse's eyes.
Halvor was just drying out
by the stove when we heard

a knocking out on the porch,
and there stood Jimmy's pony,
covered with ice and snow,
with a bag on her halter,
and in it a note which said
"Your boy is safe at the school."

## A Man's Voice:

We lived in Looking-Glass Valley
in Platte County. It snowed so hard
you couldn't see the porch posts
three feet from the door. Hundreds
of sheep and cattle froze to death,
drifting before the wind
and catching up in fences.
A neighbor lost sixty hogs;
they piled up on each other,
and the bottom ones smothered
while the top ones froze. People
were trading hide for supplies
that spring, as I remember.

## A Woman's Voice:

Father was ill with the mumps,
and Mother none too strong
and only nineteen. She brought
our milk-cow, Betty, right into
the dugout with us, and there,
on the following morning,
Betty gave birth to a calf
we named Rufus. But our oxen,
out in the straw shed, perished.
As the snow drifted in, it seems
they kept tramping it down
until their backs were up against
the rafters. After the storm,

nearby, we also found
the body of an antelope.

## A Man's Voice:

When the wind and snowstorm struck,
our teacher dismissed the school
and told us to get for home.
My older brother and I
started out on our horse,
but the snow was so blinding
we soon were lost. We let the horse
loose, taking the blanket with us,
and walked with the wind, hoping
to find some sort of shelter.
We finally had to dig
down into a drift, wrapping
the blanket around us. Billy
died in the night. I thought he
was only asleep. At dawn,
I dug out, finding that we
were in sight of the home place.
They had to cut my feet off.

## A Man's Voice:

As the news of the storm got out,
it seems that the papers
needed a heroine, someone
to fix in the public eye
as an example of courage
out on the savage prairies.
They chose Minnie Mae Freeman,
a girl in her teens who taught school
in a soddy near Ord.
When the wind came up that day,
it blew in the door, then ripped off
a good part of the roof.
Minnie lined up the children
and led them out into the storm
hand-in-hand, sixteen of them.
They reached a house a half-mile off,
and were saved. Minnie got mail
from all over the country,
to her great embarrassment.

## A Woman's Voice:

I was embarrassed all right!
Of all of the children saved,
and there were many, they chose
my school to make a story of.
Besides, the papers, looking
for romance, wrote of a man,
supposed to be my fiance,
that I hardly knew. The *Bee*,
our paper there in Ord,
sold pictures of the school
for a dollar apiece,
and people from everywhere
sent me letters and cards
and told me their troubles.

## A Man's Voice:

The searching parties started out
early the following day,
for fear that the prairie wolves
would get to the bodies first
and disfigure their faces.
We found one of our neighbors
caught up in a barbwire fence
only a few yards from his barn.
He'd been too weak from the cold,
or so we guessed, to pull free,
and was covered with ice.
We had to cut through the wire
to pull his body loose.

## A Woman's Voice:

The first thing we noticed that day
was the wind in the maples.
In the school, just before
the storm hit, a few small birds
thudded against the windows
as if fleeing from something.
Father took all of us home
in a bobsled with a box,
drawn by our blind mare, Sis.
We huddled down in the bottom
under some straw, letting the horse
find her own way home. That night,
all of the pupils slept at our house,
three to a bed. Mother put out
big cornshuck ticks for us.

## A Man's Voice:

I don't remember the name
of our teacher, but she was
scarcely more than a girl.
She knew enough to tell us
we weren't to leave the school
till someone came to get us.
Some of the big boys bragged
that they could make it for sure,
but she wouldn't budge; just stood
at the door with folded arms
and a switch. Any one
of those boys could have tossed
her over a shoulder
and carried her a mile
without breaking a sweat, but they
respected her, and did just what
she told them to. Through the night,
we kept that cannonball stove
as red as a cherry
by burning coal and corncobs,

while the little children slept
covered with coats on benches.
The teacher told us stories
and read from the Bible
until our parents came for us.
I wonder what her name was.

## A Woman's Voice:

We were out of flour for bread,
and Father went to a neighbor's
to borrow some, but he got
off the road coming back
and wandered out over
the prairie. After a spell,
he fell over a stone
and knew he was in the quarry
to the south of our place.
He made it home from there.
When he came through the door
he was covered with ice,
with that flour-pail still in his hand.

## A Man's Voice:

Early in the evening
of February the fourth,
a fellow came to the door
to tell us somebody'd found
the body of my cousin.
A pitchfork handle and his cap
were sticking out of the snow.
It was no small job
digging him out. The snow
was packed around him hard.
We did the job of digging
by the light of a lantern,
and got the body home
a little after sunrise.
He was twenty years old.

## A Woman's Voice:

That spring, when the weather warmed,
there were gangs of men who traveled
from place to place, skinning
dead cattle by the thousands.
In later years, whole trainloads
of bones were shipped east, flatcars
with bones stacked up like brush,
all from that one great storm.

But some of the animals lived
through it all as if by magic.
About three weeks after the storm,
one day, walking to school,
we saw what we thought was a stick
wiggling around in a snowbank,
and there was a turkey
frozen into a drift, poking
its head out. It had been there
all that time, living on grasses
and the water from melting snow.

## A Man's Voice:

I spent that night in a shed
I'd stumbled upon in the wind,
a straw-roofed dugout. My horse
came right in with me. At dawn,
I woke to find old Danny
chewing his way through the roof
and the snow pouring in
over his head. What a storm
that was! All of the game
was covered—the prairie chickens
crowded in haystacks and froze,
the rabbits were buried. Wolves

walked through the streets of our town,
howling for something to eat.

## A Woman's Voice:

I remember how in that wind
the cows' tails stuck out sideways.
We got them into the barn
after a good deal of work,
and fed and watered them.
My outfit, I think, was ideal
for going out to the barn
and back: a bandana tied
over my mouth, a big sunbonnet
with a sack doubled over
my head and pinned at the throat,
a coat with a slicker,
a pair of overalls, felt boots
under my overshoes,
and heavy mittens for my hands.

# A Woman's Voice:

Lois Mae Royce was teaching
in District 32
near Plainview, Pierce County,
Nebraska. Nine pupils were there
in the morning, but six went home
at noon and didn't return,
due to the looks of the sky.
After the storm was upon them,
the teacher realized
there was not enough fuel
for the night, so she set out
with the three small children
to walk the two hundred yards
north to her boarding place.
There was Peter Poggensee,
nine years old, and Otto Rosberg,
nine, and Hattie Rosberg,
just six. They were soon lost
in the whirling winds and snow
and sank down in the lee

of a straw stack to rest.
Before dawn the three children
were dead, huddled beside
their young teacher, who lived
but lost both of her feet
and the use of one hand.

# A Man's Voice:

One of the older boys dared
little Nels Olson to run
over across the road
just to see how cold it was,
and he did, but coming back
he couldn't see into the wind
and missed the school. He had only
a little jacket on;
no boots or hat at all.
The teacher sent some of us out
to see if we could find him,
and we tied a scarf to the fence
to help us find our way back.
But little Nels wandered past
and found the scarf and put it on.
We finally found him
and made it back to the school,
but he was badly frozen
and lost his fingers and thumbs.

## A Man's Voice:

The Indians were too smart
to be caught by a blizzard,
and only a few of them died.
They stayed warm in their lodges
and waited it out. One man
named Rough Clouds died while hunting,
though his friend and dog survived.
According to one account,
a band of Omaha came through
the town of Silver Creek
a week after the storm had passed,
carrying one of their brothers
who had frozen to death.
They were displaying his body
for a nickel a look.
They headed east toward Omaha,
intending to take the train
still farther and to show the corpse
in cities along the way.

## A Woman's Voice:

I was teaching in Kansas—
Cloud County. Next morning,
when I got to the schoolhouse,
the door was standing open.
Snow had put out the fire
in the stove, and everything
was covered with white. I got
shovel and broom and swept up good,
and school was called on time.

## A Woman's Voice:

Father turned over the wagon
and crawled in under it
for the night. When he got home,
we cut off his buffalo boots,
put his feet in cold water,
and rubbed his face with handfuls
of snow. He recovered
unharmed, but years later,
in a depot in Iowa,
I saw one not so lucky;
there was nothing left of him
but his trunk and head. Both arms,
both legs were gone. They had him
strapped in a wheelchair there,
waiting to get on the train.

# A Man's Voice:

So go the old stories,
like wind in the long grass,
loose wind singing in fences,
wind like the white wolf
moving in over the snow.
Nobody knows now
how many died; some say
two hundred or more
in Dakota Territory,
Nebraska and Kansas.
Few records were kept;
the dead were buried at home,
in poorly marked graves
in the corners of fields.
All that was long ago,
but the wind in the hedgerow,
the wind lifting the dust
in the empty schools,
the wind which in the tin fan
of the windmill catches,
turning the wheel to the north—
that wind remembers their names.

*Other Titles by Ted Kooser*
*available from the University of Nebraska Press*

Local Wonders
Seasons in the Bohemian Alps

The Poetry Home Repair Manual
Practical Advice for Beginning Poets

*with Steve Cox*
Writing Brave and Free
Encouraging Words for People Who Want to Start Writing